Economically Developing Countries

Bangladesh

Steve Brace
ACTIONAID Education Officer

Thomson Learning
New York

Economically Developing Countries

Bangladesh
Ghana

Title page: Bananas and other goods are brought to market by boat.
Contents page: Pumping water from a tube well.

Acknowledgments
The publishers would like to thank the following for allowing their photographs to be reproduced in this book: ACTIONAID 5, 12 (bottom), 13, 16, 18, 21, 22, 28, 29, 30, 31, 32, 33, 34, 35, 36, 37, 40, 43, 45; Eye Ubiquitous 12 (top, David Cumming), 41 (Jim Holmes); Jim Holmes 4, 9, 11, 15, 16, 17, 25, 26, 39, 44, 45; Panos Pictures 7 (Jim Holmes), 23 (Liba Taylor), 42 (B. Klass); Ann and Bury Peerless 1, 3, 8; Popperfoto 19, 20. Artwork by Peter Bull (6, 10, 14, 20, 24, 27, 38, 41).

This book has been produced in association with ACTIONAID. ACTIONAID works with some of the poorest children, families, and communities in 20 countries in Africa, Asia, and Latin America. Through both long-term development programs and emergency relief, it aims to help people secure lasting improvements in their quality of life.

First published in the
United States in 1995 by
Thomson Learning
115 Fifth Avenue
New York, NY 10003

First published in Great Britain in 1994 by
Wayland (Publishers) Limited

Library of Congress Cataloging-in-Publication Data
Brace, Steve.
 Bangladesh / Steve Brace
     p.   cm.—(Economically developing countries)
 Includes bibliographical references and index.
 ISBN 1-56847-243-9
 1. Bangaldesh—Juvenile literature. [1. Bangladesh.]
I. Series
DS393.4.B73   1995
954.92—dc20   94-27843

Printed in Italy

Contents

Introduction

In Dhaka's slums, few people have running water, electricity, or proper sanitation.

Bangladesh means "land of the Bangla-speaking people." Between the twelfth and eighteenth centuries the area that is now Bangladesh was one of the most prosperous regions in the Indian subcontinent. Its thriving economy was based on cotton farming and the production of cloth. Today, Bangladesh is the twelfth-poorest country in the world.

Yet not everyone there is poor. Some people are wealthy with affluent lifestyles. However, 86 percent of the population lives in poverty. Many people have to survive on as little as 75 cents per day. As well as lacking money, poor people also lack resources such as farmland and access to services such as schools or health centers.

Because of this poverty, Bangladesh has a low level of development. Development measures the standard of living of a place. For example, development can show whether people can make choices in their lives, provide for their families, and build a prosperous and secure future. Different groups are working to promote development in Bangladesh. They include the Bangladeshi

The lush, green rice crop grows easily on the fertile soil. Despite the rich farmland, more than 90 million Bangladeshi people live in poverty.

government, local charities, international organizations such as the World Bank, rich countries, and international charities.

While Bangladesh is not a rich country, it has fertile farmland and a resilient and resourceful population. People may be poor, but this does not keep them from trying to make a better life for themselves and their families.

> *Life is hard and I never have a moment's rest. It's my own hard work, my knowledge, and my skills that keep the family going.*
> **– Sobura Katum (right)**

The Natural Environment

Bangladesh is located in the northern corner of the Bay of Bengal and is crossed by the Tropic of Cancer. It has a land area of 55,598 square miles, which is slightly larger than Wisconsin.

A typical Bangladeshi scene would include low-lying flat land, tree-fringed fields, small embankments, and an occasional *bari* (buildings grouped in small homesteads) all crisscrossed by many river channels. For most of the year the landscape is a lush green, but the fields turn gold before the rice harvest.

Bangladesh has three large rivers that originate in the much higher land of India to the north.

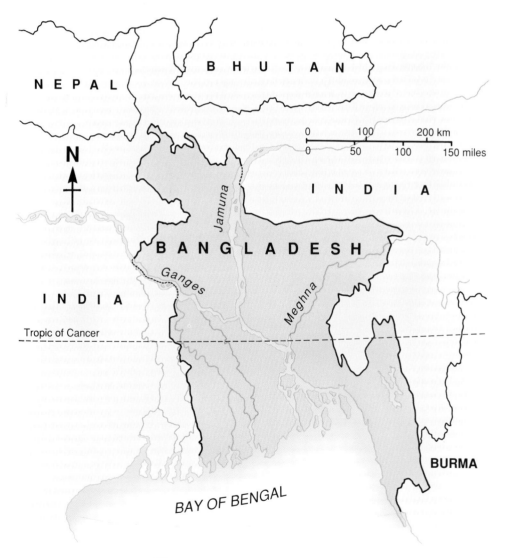

Rivers can both erode and deposit new land. This family's home may soon fall into the river as the land beneath it is washed away.

LANDSCAPE

The landscape has been formed by Bangladesh's growth as a delta. A delta is created when a river runs into the sea and deposits the sediment, or soil, it is carrying. If the sea does not wash the sediment away new land is created.

Bangladesh's delta has grown at the confluence, or meeting place, of three huge rivers: the Padma (Ganges), Jamuna (Brahmaputra), and Megna. At one point, the joined rivers form a channel 10 miles wide. In total they drain about 800,000 square miles of Indian, Nepali, and Bangladeshi land. Over many thousands of years these rivers have deposited millions of tons of sediment in the Bay of Bengal, creating the mainland delta that forms Bangladesh. This process is continuing and every year new islands and sandbars appear in the river channels. This new land is called *char* land.

As a result of Bangladesh's growth as a delta, the land is flat and low lying. There are few areas of land higher than 30 feet above sea level; many areas stand only a few inches above the water. What the rivers give they can also take away. Unless rivers have high banks, which few do, they usually change their course every two to three years. This erodes the land.

7

CLIMATE

Bangladesh has a monsoon climate, characterized by a season of heavy rains. Between July and October Bangladesh receives 100 inches of rainfall. Compare this to Washington State's 38 inches of rain and London's 24 inches distributed over the whole year.

The climate during the year in Bangladesh breaks down into three seasons:

March to June Hot and dry. Temperatures can reach 95°F before the onset of the monsoon rains.

July to October Hot and wet. Temperatures are around 85°F. Heavy monsoon rains.

November to February Cooler and dry. Temperatures drop to around 77°F. Little rainfall.

CLIMATE IN DHAKA			
Month	Temperature(°F)		Rainfall
	Max	Min	(inches)
Jan	78	55	0.5
Feb	82	59	1.25
March	91	68	2.5
April	92	74	5.5
May	91	76	10
June	90	78	13
July	89	79	13.25
Aug	88	79	13.5
Sept	90	79	9.25
Oct	89	75	5.5
Nov	84	68	1.25
Dec	79	57	0.5

During the dry season, before the monsoon, few crops can be grown. Cattle, which only the richer farmers can afford, must survive on what little grass remains.

8

This water pump and house have been built on raised mounds of earth in order to escape the floods of the monsoon season.

FLOODING

Bangladesh's landscape and climate combine to make it vulnerable to flooding. On such a low-lying landscape a small rise in river or tidal levels can easily cause flooding.

The risk of flooding is particularly high during the monsoon. One quarter of Bangladesh can be covered by just six inches of water, the flood lasting for several weeks. Some floods are a necessary part of the farming cycle. The monsoon floods are called *barsha*, which roughly means "the normal beneficial flood of the rainy season." The *barsha* are important because they leave a layer of sediment on the fields, restoring the soil's fertility. This makes Bangladesh's farmland some of the most fertile in the world.

However, when the floods are very deep or occur at an unusual time of year they are know as *bonna*. This means a "harmful flood of abnormal depth and timing."

CYCLONES

Cyclones are formed when the sea's surface heats up to over 84°F. Then the air above the sea becomes a mass of spinning winds, reaching speeds of over 125 miles per hour. In the Bay of Bengal such conditions exist during the hot, still weather just before and just after the monsoon. Cyclones can increase flooding. They bring additional rain and sea surges, which can force a 17-foot-high tidal wave up river channels and over riverbanks, causing widespread damage.

The Human Environment

Bangladesh has a population of 110 million people, half that of the United States. Eighty-six percent of Bangladeshis live in poverty. One way of showing the level of poverty is to measure people's life expectancy. This is the average length of time a person can expect to live. Bangladesh's life expectancy is only 52 years, compared to 76 years in the United States.

Bangladesh has been called "the largest and most densely populated pocket of deep poverty in the world." This does not really describe the individual living conditions for all Bangladeshis. Most Bangladeshis are Bengali. They speak Bangla, the sixth-largest language group in the world. English, inherited from the colonial past when this area was governed by the British, is also used, mainly for commerce and business. Eighty-seven percent of Bangladeshis are Muslim, 12 percent are Hindu, and the remainder are Christian or Buddhist.

Bangladesh's currency is the taka. One taka is worth about three cents.

There are many different lifestyles, ranging from Dhaka's urban people to farmers living in remote villages.

KEY
— Main roads
++++++ Railway

Rajshahi

Dhaka

Khulna

Chittagong

BAY OF BENGAL

Numerous roads and railroads link Bangladesh's main cities and industrial areas.

Work can be divided into three main areas: farming and fishing, industry (such as factory work), and service jobs (such as office work, teaching, and shop work).

In Bangladesh 72 percent of the population work in farming and fishing, 12 percent work in industry, and 16 percent work in service jobs. However, while most people live and work in the countryside, towns and cities make an important contribution to Bangladeshi life.

Dhaka, the capital city of Bangladesh, is home to nearly seven million people.

URBAN LIFE

Only 16 percent of Bangladesh's population live in urban areas, compared to 75 percent in the United States and 86 percent in Australia.

Dhaka is Bangladesh's capital city and has a population of 6.8 million people. The city is growing rapidly and has a high population density of 2,800 people per square mile. Buildings range from the historic Muslim city center to British colonial developments, and from the large, modern parliament building to *bustees* or slums.

Many of Bangladesh's rich people live in Dhaka. A typical rich family would own a large house and a car and pay for their children to be educated in a private school. They may even send their children overseas to college. For the wealthy, Dhaka has many luxury stores. They can watch live U.S. football and baseball on a satellite station called Star TV.

A large proportion of Dhaka's population lives in the poverty of the *bustees.* Here people have limited access to running water, sanitation (sewage disposal), and electricity. Roads are not paved and buildings are constructed from any available materials, such as waste wood and tin sheets. However, even in such basic conditions people still try to take care of their homes, enjoy themselves, and improve their lives.

Some prosperous people pay to travel on rickshaws, a common form of transportation.

When I get home from school I help with the cooking, carrying water, washing the floor, and making the bed. Sometimes I play. My favorite games are blindman's buff and skipping.
    – Hasina Begum, age 10, from the
slum of Dhaka

I like gardening. I grow flowers outside the house. I grow the plants to make where I live beautiful.
    – Mohammed Firoz (right), age 12,
brother of Hasina Begum

Many children take on the responsibility of earning money. Hasina, from page 12, lives next to a factory that makes saris, where girls as young as ten years old work. Children often have to work and miss the opportunity to go to school because their wages make a valuable contribution to a family's income.

Amirul Haque is ten. He goes to school from 7 a.m. to 9 a.m., and then he works a lathe until 6 p.m. He hopes that by learning to read he can qualify as a master technician.

It is common for children to work long hours. Many – like Amirul Haque shown on the right – work in factories, while others help on the farms.

Left Even in the slums, poorer people are still trying to improve their surroundings. Mohammed Firoz's flowers will add a splash of color on the street in front of his home.

Other large towns and cities include Chittagong (1,840,000 people), Khulna (860,000), and Rajshahi (430,000).

Cities are important centers for Bangladesh's manufacturing industry, with a steel mill located in Chittagong and a shipyard in Khulna. Some international companies have set up factories in Bangladesh: Unilever, owned by British and Dutch interests, produces chemicals, detergents, toiletries, and food products. Making clothes is one of Bangladesh's main industries. Bangladesh has more than 1,100 clothes factories. The finished clothes are exported to other countries. This is very important for Bangladesh, which gets 39 percent of its export earnings from the sale of clothing.

13

RURAL LIFE

Eighty-four percent of Banagladeshi people live and work in the countryside. Farming is very important and accounts for 38 percent of the country's gross domestic product (GDP). GDP is the wealth created by a country within its borders. Bangladesh also earns foreign currency by exporting agricultural products such as jute and tea.

The main food crops grown are rice, pulses, and vegetables such as potatoes and peppers. Rice is the staple food. People eat rice most days of the year, supplemented with vegetables, pulses, and fish. Meat is rarely eaten.

The lifestyle of rural areas is closely tied to the cycle of the monsoons. The main *amon* crop of rice is planted in the monsoon season during June and July and is harvested in December. The *aus* rice crop is sown earlier in the year and harvested during the monsoon. In the dry season, *rabi* or winter crops are grown, including vegetables, pulses, and peppers.

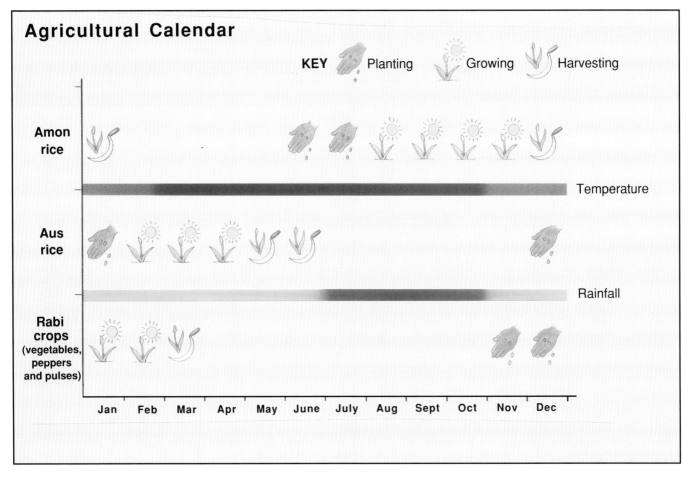

Agricultural Calendar

KEY — Planting — Growing — Harvesting

Amon rice

Temperature

Aus rice

Rainfall

Rabi crops (vegetables, peppers and pulses)

Jan Feb Mar Apr May June July Aug Sept Oct Nov Dec

Overall, Bangladesh has a population density of 1,900 people per square mile. It is the most densely populated country in the world. There is very little land to be shared among farmers, but Bangladesh is fortunate because almost all of its land is suitable for farming. Bangladesh has a more favorable "people-to-farmland" ratio than other densely populated countries such as Japan and the Netherlands.

Rice is the main food in Bangladesh where two crops are grown each year. The rice seedlings are planted by hand. It is back-breaking work.

In spite of this, Bangladesh's farmland is owned by a small number of people. Currently, 5 percent of the population owns one quarter of the land; many rich farmers own land counted in thousands of acres. However, over 60 million Bangladeshis (out of a total population of 110 million) are landless or own less than half an acre of land (roughly the size of a tennis court). In an agricultural country such as Bangladesh, the people who have no farmland often find it very hard to earn a living.

Other ways to make money in rural Bangladesh are sharecropping and wage labor.

Sharecropping   Poor farmers are loaned land by rich farmers. The poor farmers can then use the land to grow crops, but they must share the result somehow with the landowner. The poor farmer may have to buy all the seed, plow the land, tend the crops, and then give as much as half the harvest to the landowner.

Wage Labor   Many farmers work for rich farmers. Typical jobs include planting and harvesting. Sometimes wage laborers are paid in money, although it is more common to receive a percentage of the crops that they harvest.

Both men and women work for wages. However, the Muslim laws of purdah place restrictions on women working in public. When women leave their homes they veil themselves, and any paid work they perform is usually within the protection of a rich family's *bari*. However, in order to survive, very poor women sometimes break purdah, taking paid work in the fields.

Farming incomes are supplemented by making useful things to sell. Jute is an important crop because its leaves contain long fibers that are used to make rope and bags. Some people also weave mats from the leaves of the *hoogla* plant.

In rural areas people live in *baris*. A *bari* is made up of a small number of homesteads built on a raised mound of earth that protects them from flooding. *Baris* usually have a tank, like a pond, used for drinking water and washing. One *bari* may be home to 20 to 30 people. It is relatively common for poor people, who have no land of their own, to build their houses in the *bari* of a rich family.

Occasionally poor farmers can build their homes and grow crops on *char* land. However, because this is newly formed land it is always the lowest lying and will be the first land to be covered with water if there are floods.

Other occupations in rural areas include trading, road construction work, and service work such as rickshaw pulling and running stores.

Grain drying in a bari. Baris *are private, and Muslim women can work without breaking purdah.*

Fish is almost the only source of protein for many people, as they cannot afford to buy meat.

What Makes Bangladesh Poor?

There are many different reasons why Bangladesh is a poor country.

ENVIRONMENTAL REASONS

Bangladesh's people are heavily reliant on agriculture. Any disruption to the farming cycle can severely affect the people's well being.

These sluice gates were designed to remove excess flood water from the farmland, but they are broken, and the local people are not able to repair them.

Flooding can cause great difficulties. While the *barsha* floods are vital for farmers, the *bonna* floods can create much hardship. They bring flood water that is too deep, lasts too long, or arrives at the wrong time of year, and can destroy whole fields of crops and erode away land. Cyclones also cause flooding in coastal regions. The cyclone's rains, high winds, and sea surges can sweep away crops, livestock, and homes.

Such events interrupt everyday life. The problems do not stop, however, even when the waters have dropped. They can create a domino effect over the next several years. For example, farmers who have lost their crops may have to borrow money, at high interest rates, in order to buy seeds for the next planting. This can lead to people falling into debt.

17

Where there is no clean drinking water, poor people may have to drink from rivers or tanks.

DEFORESTATION

Events outside Bangladesh's borders can also increase flooding. In the Himalaya Mountains deforestation – cutting down too many trees – increases the volume of water flowing into Bangladesh's rivers. This occurs because there is not enough vegetation left to keep rainwater from flowing directly off the mountains into the rivers. Deforestation also leads to increased rates of soil erosion. The topsoil becomes sediment carried in the rivers. This can choke the river channels and therefore increase the risk of flooding.

It is not only too much water that brings problems. Too little rain can also have a negative effect on people's lives. If the monsoons do not bring enough rain, the harvest will be poor. During the dry season, few crops can be grown, and the incomes of wage laborers fall sharply.

Despite being surrounded by water – and often swamped by it – Bangladesh has a shortage of safe drinking water. People drink from rivers and tanks, or ponds, that are used by animals. As a result, water-borne diseases such as typhoid and parasitic infections are common.

HISTORICAL REASONS

Between A.D. 1100 and 1700 what is now Bangladesh was under Muslim rule. At this time Bangladesh was a very prosperous area. Some of its fertile land was used to grow cotton, and Bangladeshi-made cloth was traded widely. Unlike today, most farmers had access to land through a system of traditional land rights.

In 1757 the British East India Company took control of this region because of the raw materials it could supply to Great Britain's growing industries. It was controlled by the British for over 200 years and was known as Bengal.

British rule brought major changes. A new landowning class of people, called the *zemindars*, was created. They were allowed to charge local farmers rent for using farmland. Cash crops, grown to be sold for money rather than to be consumed, were also introduced. These included indigo (used to make dyes), sugarcane, and jute. In order to pay the rent charged by the *zemindars*, farmers had to start growing cash crops. As a result, the new crops introduced by the British replaced the traditional food crops and cotton.

Because the British wanted to use Bengal as a source of raw materials, they had no interest in allowing Bengal's industries to compete with Britain's own cotton mills. To stop any competition, the export of Bengali cotton cloth was banned, effectively closing down the Bangladeshi cloth industry.

Tying up a "drum" of jute, a cash crop introduced by the British. Jute is grown for its fibers, which are used to make sacks and rope.

New communication links were developed by the British. However, the new roads and railroads were designed to support British interests, such as the efficient export of Bangladeshi raw materials. While some Bangladeshis became rich as a result of the British rule, many lost their access to land and fell into poverty.

In 1947 India was granted its independence from Britain. At the same time the Muslim state of Pakistan was created, made up of East Pakistan, now Bangladesh, and West Pakistan, now Pakistan. A country in two parts, separated by 1,100 miles, found it difficult to form a shared identity. Also, most export earnings of this "joint" country from the sale of jute and tea were earned by East Pakistan (Bangladesh), and it appeared that new development spending was directed toward West Pakistan (Pakistan). Dissatisfaction at this situation was further increased by attempts to replace Bangla with Urdu, the language spoken in West Pakistan.

In Bengal, rule by the British brought wealth, but mainly for themselves. Most local people became worse off than before.

For more than twenty years, Bangladesh was part of Pakistan. After a civil war, Bangladesh became independent in 1971. But the war severely disrupted Bangladeshi life and used up valuable resources.

20

SOCIAL AND ECONOMIC REASONS

Bangladesh has a national debt of over $11 billion. This is money Bangladesh owes to foreign banks, governments, and international institutions. To service, or pay off, this debt costs Bangladesh 25 percent of its export earnings. These payments mean the government has less money available to invest elsewhere, such as in education or health care. In fact, Bangladesh is so short of money that over 90 percent of its spending on development programs is provided by aid from overseas.

Debt is also a problem for individuals. If disaster strikes, people often have to turn to local moneylenders who charge very high interest rates: up to 240 percent per year. This can force people into having to sell or mortgage their land and belongings.

The next five years were the worst of my life. I had absolutely nothing and was reduced to begging. It filled me with shame. My father had been an honorable man and to be dependent upon others caused me great pain.
– Sobura Katum, who had to sell her house to pay the $12 (400 taka) debt from her husband's funeral

Bustling markets provide the opportunity for farmers to buy and sell goods. They are also an important place for people to exchange news and meet one another.

Most children are needed to help with the farmwork, such as tending animals or harvesting crops. This means that they often cannot go to school to learn things that would help them build a better life.

Landless farmers have to work for rich farmers, but large numbers of farmworkers are needed only during a few months. It is also common for laborers to be hired only by people who know them. So the poor, who cannot afford the costs of travel, seldom have contacts for work outside their home area.

Landlessness can also be influenced by the Muslim Koranic laws of inheritance. When a farmer dies the land is subdivided between his sons and daughters, sons receiving a larger share than daughters. This means that as farmland is passed down from generation to generation it becomes subdivided into smaller and smaller plots.

A further influence on the availability of land is family size. The average size of a Bangladeshi family is six people, but many parents choose to have a larger family because of the chances that children may not survive into adulthood. On average, 10 percent of children die before their fifth birthday, but in very poor communities this figure reaches over 20 percent. Children are also needed to help with farmwork and to take care of elderly parents.

However, even if people had smaller families it is likely, given the present pattern of land ownership, there would still be some families without land.

Conservative attitudes toward women, particularly in rural areas, also have an effect on their involvement in development.

The women… are lagging far behind men in education. They are born and brought up behind the screen of the house, because they will surely go to hell if they show their faces to the people of the street. Instead of going to school, they read the verses from the holy Koran. These Koranic lessons reinforce their attitudes to live conservatively.

— Mukul Raman, development worker

Under the Muslim laws of purdah, a woman must veil herself when she goes out in public.

23

Measuring Development

There are many different ways of measuring how developed a country is. One method is to examine how much wealth a country produces. Gross national product (GNP) per capita (person) measures the wealth a country creates within its borders, as well as any income from trade and overseas investments, divided by the country's population. The country with the highest GNP per capita will have the most wealth available to its population and can be called the most developed country. Conversely, the country with the lowest GNP per capita has the least amount of wealth available and can be called the least developed.

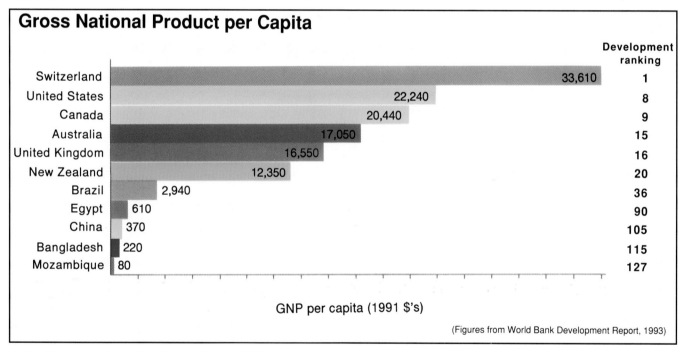

Gross National Product per Capita

Country	GNP per capita	Development ranking
Switzerland	33,610	1
United States	22,240	8
Canada	20,440	9
Australia	17,050	15
United Kingdom	16,550	16
New Zealand	12,350	20
Brazil	2,940	36
Egypt	610	90
China	370	105
Bangladesh	220	115
Mozambique	80	127

GNP per capita (1991 $'s)

(Figures from World Bank Development Report, 1993)

From this table you can see that Switzerland has the highest GNP per capita income in the world and Mozambique has the lowest GNP per capita income.

On a measure of GNP per capita, Bangladesh has the twelfth-lowest figure. This places Bangladesh as the twelfth-poorest country in the world.

However a single measure such as GNP per capita can be misleading. For example, no country in the world divides up its wealth equally among all of its people. Not everyone in the United States has exactly $22,240 to spend each year.

Measuring the numbers of people who have access to health care, clean water, and education can show how healthy and well-educated a country's population is.

Although Bangladesh is a poor country, there are a few people with enough money to pay for expensive goods such as Pepsi.

INDICATORS OF DEVELOPMENT

In Bangladesh, out of a population of 110 million people:
- 63 million people do not have access to health services
- 22 million people do not have access to safe drinking water
- 100 million people do not have access to sanitation
- 21 million children do not attend school
- 7 million children under the age of five are malnourished
- Life expectancy is 52 years

(United Nations Development Program, 1990)

Ms. Sumitra, a development worker, talks to a group of landless, poor women about the importance of health care, sanitation, and clean water.

These indicators of development illustrate the poor conditions that most Bangladeshis live in. The very miminum that people need in order to survive is called basic needs. These include food, clean water, and health care. In addition, education enables people to live better lives.

Only 35 percent of Bangladeshis can read and write. There are few schools, especially in rural areas. Even when there is widespread flooding, schools such as this one remain open whenever possible.

LOW LEVEL OF DEVELOPMENT

One development charity working in Bangladesh identifies poverty using social indicators that relate to people's lives. People have a low level of development when they experience:

- high levels of childhood deaths and malnutrition.
- high levels of unplanned births.
- high levels of illiteracy.
- limited access to clean water and good sanitation (sewage disposal).
- limited access to basic health services.
- limited access to education.
- limited access to farmland.
- limited access to credit (loans).
- high levels of soil erosion and deforestation.
- limited access to government services and legal rights.

All the figures, both economic and social, point to Bangladesh being a very poor country, but what does this level of poverty mean for individual people? How does poverty affect people's daily lives and their hopes for the future? As an example, in the next two chapters you will see how people on Bhola Island cope with poverty and how they are working to build themselves a better future.

Life on Bhola Island

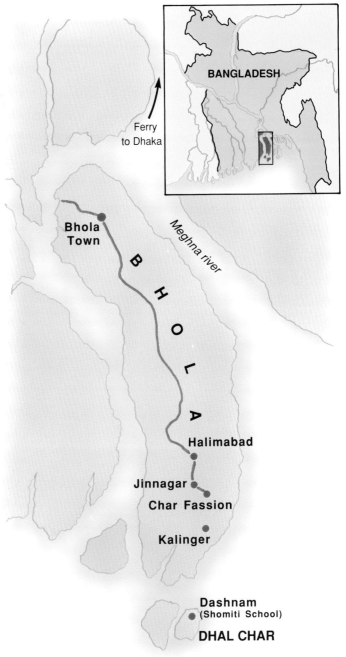

BANGLADESH

Ferry
to Dhaka

Meghna river

Bhola
Town

B H O L A

Halimabad

Jinnagar
Char Fassion

Kalinger

Dashnam
(Shomiti School)
DHAL CHAR

BAY OF BENGAL

Located in the main channel of the Padma, Jamuna, and Megna rivers, Bhola is Bangladesh's biggest island. It is over 50 miles long and 12 miles wide. The landscape is flat, no land being more than three and a half feet above sea level. A 23-foot-high embankment encircles the island, protecting it from flooding. There are few large buildings on Bhola except for schools, mosques, cyclone shelters, and the warehouses of rich traders. Bhola is home to 1.3 million people, over half of whom are landless laborers.

Bhola was once considered the "granary of Bengal" – (it was a prosperous farming region. Now the scene has changed. The majority of people are suffering and living in poverty. Only a few people have captured land titles and own land. They are living like mini feudal lords with more than 40 hectares [100 acres] of land. The wealthy live in nice corrugated sheet-metal houses. The poor people live in thatched houses.
– Mukul Rahman, development worker

Bhola shows many signs of poverty. Only 20 percent of the population is literate. Numerous villages have no one who can read and write, and many children have never set foot inside a school. Until recently clean water and health services were almost unheard of. In some areas, 80 percent of children under the age of five are undernourished.

Bhola Island is located where Bangladesh's major rivers empty into the Bay of Bengal.

One of the best ways to understand life on Bhola is to examine the lives of specific people. Roshunara is 28 years old and lives with her husband, Mohammad Yunus, in the village of Halimabad. She has had five children, although only three sons have survived. The family owns a small plot of land, which is not enough to support them, so they also have to work for other people. Roshunara's husband sells *paan*, also called betel, at a local market. People chew this green leaf, which is similar to tobacco.

When Roshunara works on a landlord's fields she receives one twelfth of all the crops she picks. One day's work picking lentils might bring her enough to feed the family for three or four meals.

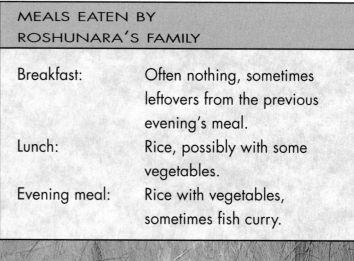

MEALS EATEN BY ROSHUNARA'S FAMILY	
Breakfast:	Often nothing, sometimes leftovers from the previous evening's meal.
Lunch:	Rice, possibly with some vegetables.
Evening meal:	Rice with vegetables, sometimes fish curry.

Inside the home of a poor family. People living on very small amounts of money can afford only straw to build their houses and a few cooking utensils.

Roshunara's children do not go to school. This is common for many of the families living here. Children often do not have time to go to school because they help their parents with farmwork. Girls also have to take care of their younger brothers and sisters. Some parents do send their children to *moktabs*, Koranic schools, where children learn to read the Koran in Arabic.

Right   *It is important for Muslim people that their children learn about their religion and read the Koran.*
Below   *Catching or selling fish is one way for people to earn money.*

My father and my mother died when I was small. Struggling hard, my aunts looked after me. I never went to school. Instead, I helped my uncle push his rickshaw and worked in a tea stall. Eight years ago I married and, having no land, built a thatched hut on the embankment. All my brothers are in a similar condition. We work on the hilsha *(fishing) boats or in the rice paddies. Sometimes I also carry fish to the market to sell.*
– Mohammad Yunus, laborer

By buying fish at the embankment and carrying them 5 miles to sell at the large Char Fassion market Mohammad earns about 15 taka (45 cents) a day.

29

Along Bhola's embankment small markets can be found. Twice a week there is a *hat*, or open market, where anyone can bring items to sell. Most people sell farm goods, like crops and livestock, or handmade items, like mats and rope. There are also permanent shops such as repair shops for rickshaws and radios, tea stalls, and restaurants.

Bhola has very basic communications. The island is linked to the mainland by ferry, taking 17 hours to reach Dhaka, the capital. There is one *pucca*, or good, concrete road running from Bhola Town to the south of the island. A bus service has been running since 1926, although most people have to walk because they cannot afford the bus fare. Other means of transport include bicycle, rickshaw, and (for the rich) motorcycle.

But there is more to life than work. There are festivals in which the whole community takes part. During one of these animals are slaughtered, and rich families share meat between themselves and local poor people. For many people, such as Roshunara, this festival will be one of the few times during the year that they eat meat.

A food stall at the hat, *or market, in Char Fassion.*

Bhola Island's one good road stands out above the flat landscape. All other roads are made of dirt, so traveling around is difficult.

Development on Bhola Island

Poverty on Bhola Island is acute. People struggle to provide for their families and have few chances to improve their lives. So what can be done to overcome poverty?

As an outsider it is easy to make snap judgments about what would be best, but any development work needs to be based on the real experiences of the people concerned. After all, it is people living on Bhola Island who are the experts at dealing with poverty.

A charity called ACTIONAID has been supporting development work on Bhola Island since 1983. Its aim is to run long-term development projects with poor communities. By talking to poor people ACTIONAID realized that a lack of financial resources is one of the main obstacles that keep people from improving their living standards. Poor people in Bangladesh cannot go to a bank and take out a loan. Instead, their only major source of money is to risk falling into debt with private moneylenders. If the poor had more money, they could invest it in activities to increase their incomes.

There are more than 600,000 landless families on Bhola Island. Development work aims to improve their living standards.

31

To overcome the poor's lack of financial resources, a savings and credit program was started. This program is run through 360 *shomiti* groups. The Bangla word *shomiti* translates as "club" or "association." Each *shomiti* is composed of 20 people and meets once a week. As well as the savings and credit program, these meetings also provide the opportunity for poor people to talk about their problems and share their ideas.

SAVINGS AND CREDIT

The *shomiti* groups provide the poor with access to a new source of money. Every week each member saves between two and eight taka (six and twenty cents). The savings are recorded in a savings book and placed in a bank where they earn interest. Once people have made a number of regular payments they can take out a loan from the pooled funds. The first loan people could take was 500 taka ($15), and additional loans could be up to 1,800 taka ($54). Interest on the loans is charged at 18 percent per year, which is much cheaper than the moneylenders' rates. The loans are paid back in small weekly installments.

Shomiti members are free to use their loans for any purpose. Many people use them to pay off existing high-interest debts; some buy a sack of rice to ensure that their family has regular meals; others invest in *hoogla* leaves that are used to make mats to sell.

A mat woven from hoogla *leaves will earn this woman a few taka when she sells it at the local market.*

Because of the rule of purdah, male development workers faced a problem working with local women. By dealing sensitively with the shomiti *groups, they slowly won the women's trust.*

WOMEN AND SHOMITI GROUPS

The *shomiti* groups are focused on the poorest people, so their members are mainly women. However, many women were concerned about attending because the groups led to contact with men who were strangers. As Achiya said when she heard about a new *shomiti* group, "It made my nose wrinkle and me feel ashamed. Women leaving the house and breaking the Muslim rules of seclusion! Meeting strange men like the development workers! It's not for a well brought up, respectable woman. Just because you're poor doesn't mean you have to lose your self respect." However, Ayub Ali, her husband, was not so sure. He suggested that Achiya talk to some local women who were already members. She did and three months later, reassured by their comments, she joined the *shomiti*.

For many poor people, the first step in improving their lives and gaining self-respect is to own a simple house on a small piece of land.

This is only a straw house, and we go hungry sometimes. But this is our house on our land. We couldn't do that without the shomiti. *With our first loan we bought a* tela-gar *[a hand-pulled delivery cart], which my son pulls. We could easily pay back the loan because it's in small weekly payments. With our next loan we bought one twelfth of an acre and built this house. We used to live on government land with no security and surrounded by rough types. Ever since our home in Mehendiganz was eroded away, we've dreamed of owning our own home. Now we've land and a* bari *with a proper address. No one bothered with us before; now people respect us.*

– Sakhina and Halima, members of a shomiti in the village of Jinnagar, explaining how a shomiti helped them buy land

Achiya, who was initially worried about joining a *shomiti* group, shows how loans were invested in business. With a loan of 400 taka she bought a goat. Another loan bought tires and inner tubes for the rickshaw that Ayub Ali, Achiya's husband, rented from a rich man. Everyone in the *shomiti* commented that this was strange. Why buy new tires for someone else's rickshaw? But Achiya had planned ahead. After a few weeks she took a large loan from the *shomiti*, sold the kid her goat had given birth to, and borrowed some money from another *shomiti* member. She took all this money home to Ayub Ali. Later that night he went with 2,800 taka to buy the rickshaw he used to rent. Now Ayub Ali is the proud owner of his own rickshaw. He now makes 60 to 70 taka per day, a great improvement on his previous wages.

Ayub Ali was able to buy his rickshaw only because his wife, Achiya, could borrow money from her shomiti *group. Because he now owns the rickshaw, instead of renting it from a richer man, he can now earn better wages each day.*

By October 1992 on Bhola Island, over $510,500 had been collected as savings from weekly payments of a few cents. During the same period $1,500,000 of loans had been taken out from a fund provided by the charity. Over 96 percent of people have paid back their loans, a very high rate of repayment. In total, over 16,000 landless families on Bhola Island have access to the shomiti savings and credit program. The success of this program is that the loans allow poor people to make choices in their lives and to take concrete steps toward improving their living standards.

EDUCATION

A common statement made by the *shomiti* members is, "If our children can read and write, they won't suffer the way we have."

Apurba Sundari, her daughter, and her granddaughter, Rupoti. Learning to read will mean that Rupoti will have more opportunities in the future than the older women have had.

I didn't learn to read and write; I've been like a cow, or a beast of burden. I'm very happy it's not going to be like that for my daughter and granddaughter.
– Apurba Sundari

Child literacy was the first activity we wanted to start with profits [from the shomiti *loans]. It will be very helpful when my daughter Rupoti becomes literate. When she gets married she will be treated better.*
– Apurba's daughter

Members of a *shomiti* group decided to support a school. The headmaster of Dashnam Shomiti School is Jogo Bondha Roy. His four teachers provide five classes a day for 210 children, ages five to fifteen. The teachers are paid about 200 taka ($6) a month from funds raised by the *shomiti* group.

Jogo Bondha Roy, the headmaster of a shomiti *school. Although there is very little money available to run the school, he is determined to make it succeed.*

I am very poor and I don't know how I will keep going. But if I stop, the people in this area will lose their great respect for me as a headmaster. I am the one who built this school up from scratch, so I will not leave.

– Jogo Bondha Roy

The impact of these *shomiti* schools has been great. In all, 70 schools and child learning centers (classes running in the morning or evening so children can still work on the farm) have been started on Bhola Island. Among landless farmers here, literacy was often less than 3 percent. Over a number of years the schools have almost doubled this figure to 5.5 percent.

Increasing child literacy has also had domino effects, such as improving crop yields. For example, children can now read the instructions on fertilizer sacks and tell their parents the correct dose for the crops. Increased child literacy also encourages parents to learn to read and write for themselves. Mirroring the creation of the *shomiti* schools, 51 adult learning centers have been started.

End of the day at a shomiti *school. All over the island,* shomiti *groups are helping to start schools that educate both children and adults.*

37

CLEAN WATER

Although water from tanks and rivers is often contaminated, Bangladesh does have large supplies of fresh water. However, it is 825 feet underground. To reach this safe water, tube wells are being built in many places.

To construct a well a one-inch-wide hole is drilled 825 feet deep to reach the aquifer, the underground water supply. A thin rubber tube is then dropped down into the hole. At ground level, a concrete slab is laid and the pump mechanism set in place. The finished tube well will provide fresh water for up to 50 years.

To ensure that people feel ownership over a tube well they have to contribute 1,000 taka ($30) toward the cost of a well. The local community also has to provide meals and accommodation for the workers who dig the well.

The location of a tube well is decided in consultation with local people. However, to ensure that the poorer people have access to the water, development workers have the final say. This prevents the new wells from being taken over by wealthier people. An example of this is shown by the experience of Kalinger village.

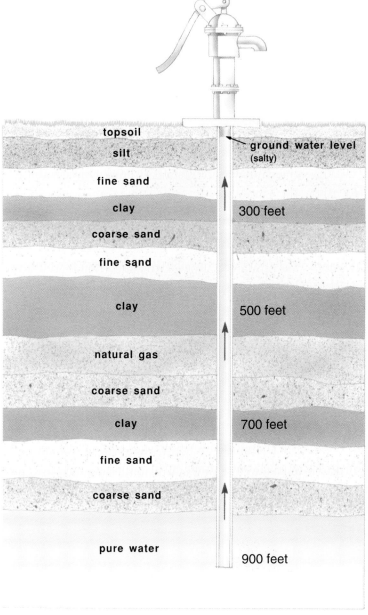

Safe drinking water is located 825 feet below the surface of the ground. A hole is drilled through the earth, a pipe is dropped down the hole, and the pump at the top brings up the water.

Having a well here has been great for everybody! Now we can use it regularly. We have no fear of sickness. The well is good for the strength of the village.

– Mohammed Nasim Haidan

38

KALINGER VILLAGE: A TALE OF TWO WELLS

The chairman of Kalinger persuaded the government to dig a tube well next to the mosque. However, 56 poor families lived at the other end of the village. It took women from these families over an hour to collect water from the mosque's well. A new tube well was dug to provide water for the poor families at the other end of the village. Josneara explained how the new well was more useful. She said, "Men don't understand. We women fetch the water; men never think of what we go through to get it. They think of the mosque, of course, and that's right: men must wash before they pray. My husband voted for the chairman, and he's proud of the chairman's well. But my friends and I, we like our new well here!"

More than 1,000 tube wells have been dug on Bhola Island. This has provided a safe source of drinking water for more than 200,000 people.

By taking water for drinking and cooking from the tube well, people know that they are drinking safe water that is free of diseases.

HEALTH

Discussion in *shomiti* groups identified tetanus as a major disease affecting local people. The Bangladeshi government and UNICEF were already running a countrywide immunization program. The *shomiti* groups organized and encouraged members to receive immunizations from this program. In all, 171,000 women have been immunized against tetanus and 104,000 children for a range of diseases including diptheria and polio. Immunization is now very well accepted by members who now know the names of the major diseases and the dates when booster shots are needed. The neighbors of *shomiti* members are also beginning to recognize the value of immunization for the health of their children.

Health education messages also reach families through their children who attend *shomiti* schools. One mother, talking about her son who attends a *shomiti* school, said, "He tells me we must eat more vegetables and reminds me to cover the rice to keep away the flies that spread disease."

Health education has also meant the creation of a training program for traditional birth attendants. These women are similar to midwives and help women give birth at home as there are no hospitals on Bhola. Their training course highlights the role of hygiene and how to reduce the risk of infection.

The savings and credit program has played an important role in improving people's nutrition. Undernourishment in children under five years old can be identified by measuring the circumference of a child's upper arm. A child is said to be undernourished if his or her arm measures less than 5 1/4 inches.

During the first year of many *shomiti* groups, the numbers of

An injection sometimes hurts, but it will protect this child from killer diseases such as diphtheria and tetanus.

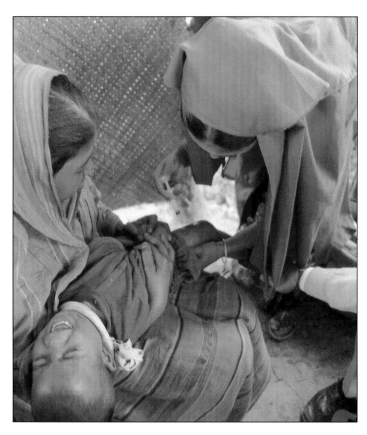

40

Food is plentiful just after the harvest, but when people's food stocks run down over the rest of the year, many poor families have to miss meals.

undernourished children fell from 50 percent to 20 percent for two reasons. First, some members used a loan to buy stocks of food such as a sack of rice, which meant their families were less likely to miss meals. Second, by investing in business activities, other families had a new source of income that could be spent on food for the family.

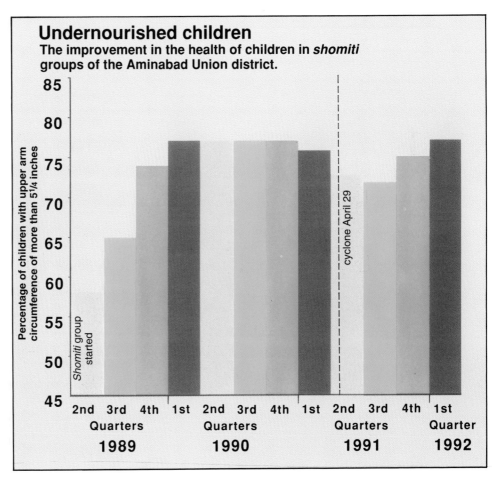

Undernourished children
The improvement in the health of children in *shomiti* groups of the Aminabad Union district.

Percentage of children with upper arm circumference of more than 5¼ inches

Shomiti group started

cyclone April 29

	2nd	3rd	4th	1st	2nd	3rd	4th	1st	2nd	3rd	4th	1st
Quarters				Quarters				Quarters			Quarter
1989				**1990**				**1991**			**1992**

41

CYCLONES

During the night of April 29, 1991, Bhola's development gains were nearly lost when a cyclone missed Bhola by only 18 miles, passing to the south of the island. The cyclone eventually crashed into the Bangladeshi coast near Chittagong, killing 138,000 people and flooding a wide area of land. Bhola was lucky. Its embankment was not breached and there were no deaths from the cyclone, although property, crops, and animals were swept away.

A cyclone's winds and the flooding it causes can sweep across Bangladesh's low-lying land, destroying crops, killing animals, and knocking down all but the strongest buildings.

We heard news of the cyclone from the radio. The sky was heavy with clouds and wind, so we took shelter in the cyclone shelter. There were a lot of people and hardly any space to stand up. We spent the whole night in the shelter. I saw the water and it was very high. We left at seven o'clock in the morning. We went back to our home and found nothing. Our cattle were all dead. We searched for our home but there was nothing to recover; everything was gone.

– Abdul Kader, farmer

In response to the cyclone damage, an interest-free loan of 600 taka ($18) was immediately released into the account of each *shomiti* member. This loan was to be paid off over two years. By taking these loans *shomiti* members were able to start rebuilding their lives, rather than being concerned about falling into debt. The loans also allowed people to reduce the long-term effect of the cyclone, particularly during the last half of the year. The childhood nutrition graph on page 41 shows how the percentage of undernourished children did rise after the cyclone. However, the loans provided a safety net and rates of undernourishment did not rise to the earlier high levels.

The Bangladeshi government aims to provide cyclone shelters for everyone. In the long term, cyclone shelters will protect people. However, at $70,000 each, they are very expensive to build. Cheaper and more locally based alternatives are available. On the island of Dal Char, south of Bhola, many people survived the cyclone by sheltering in the *shomiti* school. The cost of reinforcing school buildings so they can double as cyclone shelters is less than building shelters from scratch.

Poverty still exists on Bhola Island, but development projects are enabling poor people to improve their conditions. By having access to resources and support, the poor are able to make choices leading to a more secure future for themselves and their families.

This shomiti *school on Dal Char has been built on stilts to keep it above the flood level, and its walls have been reinforced to protect it from strong winds. It now doubles as a cyclone shelter.*

The Future of Bangladesh

Senior Bangladeshi economist Rehman Sobban said, "Bangladesh has, at low levels of basic need, the capacity to feed, clothe, house, educate, and provide medical care to its population." The challenge is to turn this capacity into reality for the people of Bangladesh.

A shop selling rice and pulses. New types of seeds are now allowing farmers to get higher yields (to harvest more grain from the same amount of land).

Across the whole country improvements are taking place. In agriculture, the introduction of high yielding varieties (HYV) of rice and the use of irrigation and fertilizers have improved farm output. By 1989 over 30 percent of Bangladesh's rice paddies were planted with HYV rice, and irrigation covered 6,200 square miles of land. Some people have argued that these changes in growing rice are too expensive for everyone to be able to use, although there is evidence to show that poor people can gain some benefits.

There are also large-scale projects aimed at controlling the annual flooding of the rivers and protecting Bangladesh from cyclone damage.

Bangladesh is helped to run these projects by international banks and rich countries. In 1993 the United States gave over $120 million in aid, Britain gave over $82 million, Canada gave $70 million, and Australia gave $15 million. Rich countries are important not only for Bangladesh's financial support, but also because they are a

Life in Bangladesh is not always a struggle. Here, a group of Hindus is celebrating a festival.

market for their exports. If changes are made to trading arrangements, Bangladesh may be able to earn more money from its exports. This could benefit both farmers and people working in Bangladesh's clothing factories.

However, whatever actions are taken to promote development, they must take the needs of the poor into consideration. You have seen how poor families on Bhola Island have started to secure real improvements in their lives. It is important to remember that poor people have hopes for the future and are prepared to work to achieve a better life.

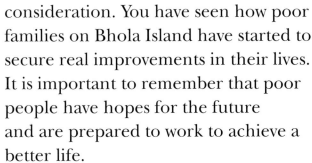

Poor people, like Mohammed Idris Miah, do not have to live in absolute poverty. When given very basic help, they can make positive changes to achieve a better life.

My ambition is to improve my standard of life. Somehow I will get some assets through doing hard work. I shall wear better clothes and eat better meals.

– Mohammed Idris Miah (left), from Bhola Island

45

Glossary

Amon   The main rice crop, which is sown before the monsoon.

Aquifer   A layer of rock that holds water.

Aus   A rice crop sown during the monsoon.

Bangla   The language spoken in Bangladesh.

Bari   A group of homes in the countryside.

Barsha   The normal beneficial floods of the rainy season.

Bonna   Harmful floods that do not occur at the usual time of year.

Bustee   An area of slum buildings.

Char **land**   New land formed in river channels.

Confluence   Where two or more rivers join together.

Cyclone   A system of very strong winds blowing inward in a spiral.

Deforestation   Cutting down large numbers of trees to leave bare land.

Delta   An area of land at the mouth of a river formed from soil and sediment washed down by the river.

Erosion   The gradual wearing away of soil by wind or water.

Export earnings   The money a country earns by selling its products to foreign countries.

Gross domestic product (GDP)   The money a country makes within its borders.

Gross national product (GNP)   The money a country makes within its borders plus any money it makes from trade and overseas investments.

High yielding varieties (HYV)   Varieties of rice that are bred to give an improved harvest.

Hindu   Someone who follows Hinduism, the main religion of India. They believe in reincarnation and many gods.

Hoogla   A plant with long, tough leaves that can be woven into mats.

Islam   The religious faith of the Muslims. They believe in one god, Allah, and in Muhummad as Allah's prophet.

Life expectancy   The average length of time a person can expect to live.

Literate   Able to read and write.

Moktab   A school where children learn to read the Koran in Arabic.

Monsoon   The heavy rains that fall between July and October.

Paan/**betel**   A green leaf, similar to tobacco, that when chewed gives a stimulating effect.

Pulses   Edible seeds of plants such as peas, beans, and lentils.

Purdah   Islamic laws that require a woman to veil herself when she goes outside her home.

Rabi   A winter crop, such as vegetables.

Shomiti   A savings and credit group.

Tank   A pond used for drinking water and washing.

UNICEF   United Nations Children's Fund.

Urdu   The official language of Pakistan.

World Bank   A bank that lends money to developing countries to help reduce poverty by promoting long-term economic growth.

Zemindars   A group of landlords, introduced by the British, who were allowed to charge farmers rent.

Further Information

Addresses

ACTIONAID
Hamlyn House
Archway, London N19 5PG
England

CARE
660 First Avenue
New York, NY 10016

OXFAM America
115 Broadway
Boston, MA 02116

UNICEF
1 UN Plaza
New York, NY 10017

Office of the Prime Minister
   of Bangladesh
Dhaka
Bangladesh

Bangladesh Embassy
2201 Wisconsin Avenue NW
Washington, DC 20007

Books

Cumming, David. *The Ganges Delta and Its People.* People and Places. New York: Thomson
Learning, 1994.

Knapp, Brian. *Drought.* World Disasters. Milwaukee: Raintree Steck-Vaughn, 1990.

Knapp, Brian. *Storm.* World Disasters. Milwaukee: Raintree Steck-Vaughn, 1990.

Lauré, Jason. *Bangladesh.* Enchantment of the World. Chicago: Childrens Press, 1992.

McClure, Vimala. *Bangladesh: Rivers in a Crowded Land.* New York: Macmillan Children's Book
Group, 1989.

Index

Numbers in **bold** refer to illustrations